YEARS,
MONTHS,
AND DAYS

YEARS, MONTHS, AND DAYS

LUKE HATHAWAY

poems

BIBLIOASIS
Windsor, ON

First edition 2018
Second edition 2025
2 4 6 8 10 9 7 5 3 1

ISBN 978-1-77196-669-6 (print)

Readied for the press by Daniel Wells
Copyedited by Emily Donaldson
Second edition designed and readied
for the press by Vanessa Stauffer

Published with the generous assistance of the Canada Council for the Arts, which last year invested $153 million to bring the arts to Canadians throughout the country, and the financial support of the Government of Canada. Biblioasis also acknowledges the support of the Ontario Arts Council (OAC), an agency of the Government of Ontario, which last year funded 1,709 individual artists and 1,078 organizations in 204 communities across Ontario, for a total of $52.1 million, and the contribution of the Government of Ontario through the Ontario Book Publishing Tax Credit and the Ontario Media Development Corporation.

PRINTED AND BOUND IN CANADA

CONTENTS

PROLOGUE

O you who know my will
but do not understand it
and must be driven still
in restlessness, or stranded,
your soul will not be still
until you are resigned
how gentle is your friend
and kind.

I can see the place,
near to me as you are,
clearly as your face,
but I cannot go there.

you see I've come
so very far
from nothingness
that now I can
not see it for

carry my
come to me
cross with your
burdens

by your light lead me
for I am blinded

alone
I ask
who shrives
the heart

I.

YEARS

Now we lay to rest,
covering with earth,
one whose birthright is
to return to dust.

You who follow, follow:
what you are I was;
what I am you'll be,
leading where I lead.

come to think
how well a coffin
comes at last
to fit a person

Before you were
I did not grieve you;
now you are not
I cannot leave you.

Clay house
out worn,
old bones
new born.

If it kills me
I will kill
the death in me
before it kills me.

Death we inherit,
one from another,
so we pass on,
one to another.

How do
you break
a house
of earth?

As if I had nothing,
as if I were naked.

That I
who is
but clay
should feel
such joy.

II.

MONTHS

A man
goes here
and there
to sow
the seed
falls here
and there
the birds
go here
and there
to eat
the seed
the man
goes forth
to sow.

we are one,
branch and fruit,
fruit and vine,
vine and root

a spring of pure water,
a sprig of new growth,
a branch bearing fruit,
a patch of good earth

lucky us
having lots
let us not
us forget
who do not
have enough
and do not
us forget

stay in the garden,
here where we cannot

light locked
against
us, who
will let
us in?
the lamb
we kill
with our
own hands

Summer to autumn,
how do we travel,
autumn to winter,
one to another,
winter to springtime,
how do we travel,
springtime to summer,
one to another.

The harvest that we saw,
so vivid in our minds,
is vanished from the fields
and what we didn't see,
or didn't think we sowed,
it blooms abundantly.

All: hay,
men, too,
must die,
made new.

Take this and eat it,
this is my flesh and blood,
flesh being grass, grass being bread.

Open sky
holding rain:
spring your locks,
give us rain;
lavish earth
keeping seed:
spring your locks,
give us bread.

Sewn with death
can I oppose
the chosen number
of my days?

The grain
stands blessed
in fields
where it
is raining.

III.

DAYS

no sooner the morning,
the shadowing night

Night falls,
we tire;
all
retire;
O,
my soul,
get thee
to higher
ground.

take my hand,
marrow-deep,
make an end,
sorrow, sleep

as easy as passing
from morning to evening,
from evening to morning,
I think it no journey

In holy darkness I go in:
speak you now let me be still.

It is risen,
it is spoken:
night concluded
morning broken.

Day breaks, arise,
the morning star
will guide us now:
awake, my soul,
and do not stop
until you find
the little child.

dawn in sunset,
fruit in blossom,
man in infant,
it is written

What happened, happens,
what was, is,
agony, and bliss.

O wake
me from
the sleep
of being
sure.

THREE HYMNS

take note
did God

did God
your God

your God
from heaven

from heaven
itself

itself
call you

call you
to take note

O stay with your Grace,
with me, Holy Word;

O stay with your Word,
with me, Holy Light;

O stay with your Light,
with me, Holy Blessing;

O stay with your Blessing,
with me, Holy Shelter;

O stay with your Shelter,
with me, Holy Supplicant;

stay with your Supplicant,
me, Holy God.

Go your way united;
the god of unity
has heard your united prayer to go your way united.

Go your way in peace;
the god of peace
has heard your peaceful prayer to go your way in peace.

Go your way in love;
the god of love
has heard your loving prayer to go your way in love.

Go your way in joy;
the god of joy
has heard your joyful prayer to go your way in joy.

AFTERWORD

First printed in the community now known as Kitchener, Ontario, in 1836, *Die Gemeinschaftliche Liedersammlung* is a collection of Protestant hymns compiled for the use of Ontario Mennonites. According to Harold S. Bender, it was most likely edited by farmer, teacher, preacher, and author Bishop Benjamin Eby (1785–1853). Reprinted many times since then, the book is still in use; it is, as far as I know, the exclusive hymnal used in the Old Order Mennonite meeting houses of Waterloo Region.

Hymns are, among other things, poems: they are recognized as such by at least one Old Order author, Isaac R. Horst, who, in his *Lieder Sammlung Commentary,* refers to the authors of these hymns as poets. The *Liedersammlung* may not be the first book of poems ever published in Waterloo Region, but its continuous weekly, if not more frequent, use in Waterloo Mennonite homes and meeting houses for the last 180 years may well make it the most-read book of poems ever published in the region. Its poems were not written here, but several lifetimes' worth of reading, singing, and sharing has commingled the lyrics and melodies with this region's weather, its seasons, its rhythms of labour and rest. (That said, 180 years—a long time in the span of the printed word—is an eyeblink in the span of human habitation in this area: Geoff Martin's essay "From the Banks of the Grand" is a salutary reminder.)

I grew up on the fringes of Waterloo Region, the child of American immigrants who brought with them their own books—not hymnals, as was the case with the Mennonite migrants to the area two centuries earlier, but secular *vade mecums:* the poetry of Emily Dickinson, Robert Frost, and Wallace Stevens, some of which my mother, an English teacher, knew by heart; the textbooks on mathematics and systems theory that would form the subject matter of the courses my father would teach at the University of Waterloo. Growing up in this secular household, I in some sense shared very little with the Old Order children who were my neighbours (and who, as weekly hymn-singers, must have known by heart more verse, at the age of seven, than I do now). Yet in other ways we had much in common: the landscape, the weather, the turn of the seasons. The experience of growing up and growing older. The human grapple that is our coming to terms with death and birth.

My own growing up took me away from Waterloo Region, but in the summer of 2015 I returned—as an adult, a poet—for a three-week-long artist residency. With the other artists involved, I walked and talked and spent time at various sites around the town of St Jacobs, where the residency was based. On the afternoon of a Friday in May we found ourselves uneasy visitors to the Old Order cemetery on Three Bridges Road, beside the Conestogo Meeting House. Uneasy, because we were living people visiting the dead, and all the more so because we were outsiders here in other ways: outsiders to the Old Order Mennonite community, first and foremost; then, too—city-based artists that we now are—to the community of southern Ontario farm people with which the Mennonite community to some extent overlaps; and finally to the community of Christian faith. Some of us came from Christian families but had left the church; others, like me, were born and bred in the briar patch of secular skepticism.

The Old Order grave markers are taciturn, but, short on words they are long on numbers: the age of the deceased, whether the person recollected lived a few years or many decades, is lovingly given in years, months, and days.

Standing in the graveyard, we began to number our own days, as the hymnal admonishes *(Lass mein Herz die Tage zählen):* Matt Borland, 32 years, 5 months, and 12 days . . . ; Amanda Jernigan, 36 years, 5 months, and 17 days . . . ; Sarah Kernohan, 34 years, 10 months, and 23 days . . . ; Colin Labadie, 31 years, 1 month, and 15 days . . . Not obits, these—as I mean those ellipses to signify— but changing tallies, unfolding counts, the linear progressions of years beautifully tempered, in this tripartite accounting, by the tallies of months and days which perennially begin anew. (Where are we now? 38 years, 2 months, and 15 days, for me, as I write this.)

When we returned to the studio, Labadie, a musician and composer, began to ring the changes on those numbers, using them to create a melody, hymn-like in its key, but odd and unfamiliar in its numerically-dictated intervals: an offering, a celebration, a lament; an expression of both intimacy and disorientation.

And I went to the library, in search of words:

for a meeting-house gravestone, however taciturn, must overhear words enough—on Sunday mornings, and also on burying days. In the stacks of the library at Conrad Grebel University College in Waterloo, I found the *Liedersammlung,* a 2011 version published with facing-page, literal translations into English of the German hymns.

The poetic fragments that I created, coming out of my reading of the *Liedersammlung,* are, like Labadie's first musical meditations, expressions of both intimacy and disorientation. They are not translations so much as they are meditations on the possibility of translation, in the broadest sense: what can be carried across the boundary between languages? And—perhaps a more pressing question in my time and place—what can be carried across the boundary between religions, or between religion and secularity; between a world defined by the presence of God, and a world defined by His absence—or perhaps by other sorts of presences and Presences?

There is an imperative for separateness in the Old Order community—a resistance to the erosion of those customs and traditions that keep the community distinct *(A Separate People* is the title of one of Horst's books on Old Order traditions)—

and I realize that to some extent this must include resistance to the project of translation: certainly to the sort of loose or poetic translation (or, "meditation on the possibility of translation," as I've called it above) that forms the basis of *Years, Months, and Days.* This imperative has deep roots in Anabaptist theology, going back to the sixteenth century. And so it is with trepidation that I offer this book to the community whose hymnal and whose numerically eloquent grave markers inspired it. But I do offer it—not least to those community members whose bodies lie in the Three Bridges Cemetery and whose dates are commemorated there—in the spirit, perhaps, of Old Order writers and scholars who have put their faith in translation, literally and figuratively: the authors of the facing-page translations in my *Liedersammlung* (I list their names here, indebted as I am to their work: Ephraim D. M. Martin, Amsey W. Martin, Abram R. Bowman, Jesse W. Bowman, and Christian R. Bowman); Horst himself, who wrote textual histories of these hymns for younger generations of worshippers; the original compiler or compilers of the *Liedersammlung,* who took these old Protestant hymns and gave them life in a new place, in a new tradition. These writers and scholars knew that conscientious translation emphasizes the inimitability of an original, even as it attempts to carry something of that original across into a new context. It is my hope that readers of *Years, Months, and Days* will find in its words both a gesture of respect for the separateness of the Old Order Mennonites, and an honest attempt to carry across something of their tradition into the context of another personhood: to hear and understand, as best I can, from within my own mind, heart, body, and spirit, some of the old words that have shaped their world, and in turn been shaped by it.

In the course of working on this book, I came to realize that these old words—or their English-language relatives—have shaped me, too: unchurched though I am, the rhythms and sentiments of the hymns I sang with my lapsed-Protestant grandfather, the rosary prayers I learned from my devoutly Catholic grandmother, were laid down in me in early childhood. It was a metaphysical education, but it was also a poetic education, and as a poet, if not as a worshipper, I have stayed in the world of these teachings.

If this work is an offering to the community of the cemetery at Three Bridges, it is also an offering to the landscape of my childhood, its weather and its seasons. This is a landscape that I shared with my Old Order neighbours, and that we all share with other neighbours, human and non-human, here now, here long before us, following us here.

In the most immediate sense, this is an offering of words to music: I wrote these fragments in the first instance to present to Labadie, that he might work on them his own translation. The numerical structures, the evolving loops that characterize his music influenced the form of what is here. (The fragments without initial capitalization and terminal punctuation are themselves designed to loop.) He chose fourteen fragments from my original text, and those became the libretto for his choral piece *Years, Months, and Days,* commissioned by Inter Arts Matrix and first given life in voice by the Kitchener-Waterloo community choir Menno Singers—Mennonite, but not Old Order, and thus both outside and inside the *Liedersammlung* world—under the directorship of Peter Nikiforuk. Teach me to number my days, says the hymnal. "Griefe brought to numbers cannot be so fierce," writes Donne, "For, he tames it, that fetters it in verse."

AMANDA JERNIGAN, 2017

FURTHER READING

Bender, Harold S. "Gemeinschaftliche Liedersammlung." *GAMEO (Global Anabaptist Mennonite Encyclopedia Online)*. 1956. Web. 24 Feb. 2017.

Die Gemeinschaftliche Lieder-Sammlung. Trans. Ephraim D. M. Martin, Amsey W. Martin, Abram R. Bowman, Jesse W. Bowman, and Christian R. Bowman. N.p., 2011.

Horst, Isaac R. *Lieder Sammlung Commentary*. N.p., [199–].

—. *A Separate People: An Insider's View of Old Order Mennonite Customs and Traditions*. Waterloo, ON / Scottdale, PA: Herald Press, 2000.

Labadie, Colin. *Years, Months, and Days* [musical score]. [Kitchener, ON], 2016.

Martin, Geoff. "From the Banks of the Grand." 2011. *The New Quarterly*. Web. 19 Sept. 2017.

Official web site of the Haudenosaunee Confederacy. 2016. Web. 19 Sept. 2017.

AFTERWORD TO THE SECOND EDITION

The afterword to the first edition of *Years, Months, and Days*—reprinted here verbatim—ends with my deadname.

I wonder, as that person—the person who carried that name; the person I was then—stood in Three Bridges Cemetery, tallying the years, months, and days of their elapsing span, did they realize in just what pressing and specific ways their days were numbered?

In the event, that person—whose name is inscribed on the tombstone-grey cover of the first edition, as well—had not-long left. As I reread *Years, Months, and Days* now, I see that premonition everywhere. It is a seeker's book: the book of a person who is sick unto death.

In the summer of 2020, I died and was reborn; or, to put it in another way, in one of the vernacular languages of my time/s and place/s, I transitioned socially. In the welter of uncertainty—indeed, of desperation—I was abiding in at that time, I neglected to take notice of the date; but the Province of Nova Scotia recorded my new name in its legal register on 31 July 2021, almost a year later. In the eyes of the law, then, Amanda Jernigan survived for 42 years, 7 months, and 18 days. *Requiescat in pace*.

They say the colours on the trans flag are masc-coded blue and femme-coded pink, with the white in the middle as significant of nonbinary identity; for me the white in the middle was also the blind-blazing locus of fearful transformation:

by your light lead me
for I am blinded

Transition and transformation, radical uncertainty, aloneness, nothingness — and the bright blaze of spiritual experience. My transition had as much to do with religion as with gender dysphoria, with my deep spiritual and ethical investments as with my—vestments, with the clothes I wear.

The intensity of spiritual experience is something I think I was afraid to name in my preface to the first edition—just as I was also afraid to name the settler history of which my words were and are a part: loyal to the John Donne quotation with which I ended my afterword, I tamed my grief in numbers, to the end.

Now, when I reread these poems, I experience the abundance of blank space around them like that stripe of spectral, apocalyptic brightness that goes through the middle of the trans flag. It's everything I couldn't say, everything I didn't have words for. I have words for so much more now, and yet still the blank space of all I don't know, don't understand, expands around me.

If you are reading these poems for the first time, welcome in. If you are reading them for the second or third or . . . time, welcome back. If you are part of the communities whose book is the *Liedersammlung*, I offer you these words with humility. If you are one of the original and abiding stewards of the land on which this book was made, I acknowledge your stewardship, and offer you these words with humility. If you are a human being, I offer you these words with humility. If you are God, well, then, may the words of my mouth and the meditations of my heart be acceptable in thy sight.

LUKE HATHAWAY, 2024

ACKNOWLEDGEMENTS

The residency that gave rise to *Years, Months, and Days* was called *A Sense of Place: St Jacobs Country*. It was sponsored by Inter Arts Matrix, directed by Isabella Stefanescu, and hosted by REAP Felt Lab, St Jacobs. My fellow artists in residence, along with Labadie, were visual artist Sarah Kernohan and engineer-cum-renaissance-man Matt Borland. Without Stefanescu's thoughtful direction, and the meaningful collaboration of my fellow artists, this work would not have been made.

The text of *Years, Months, and Days* was developed under the auspices of a commission from Inter Arts Matrix and Menno Singers, and funded by a Music Commissioning Grant from the Ontario Arts Council. When Labadie and I were working in St Jacobs, a number of people took time to speak with us about their faith, their music, and/or their scholarship: my thanks to Del Gingrich of the Mennonite Story Museum; Jenny

Shantz; Esther and Wesley Weber; Leonard Enns; and Laureen Harder-Gissing, Archivist-Librarian, and Ruth Steinman, Assistant Librarian, at the Milton Good Library, Conrad Grebel-University College; as well as to Stefanie Brunner, an early reader of this text.

Thanks to my queer family, past and present, ever expanding: you are my true spiritual community; and to those with whom I break bread on the daily: Anson Haney, Ethan Haney, Melissa Marr. I am grateful, too, to John Haney, who was my partner while this work was being made; and to the composer James Rolfe, who honoured these poems with a new musical setting in 2020.

ALSO BY LUKE HATHAWAY

Groundwork: poems (Biblioasis, 2011)
All the Daylight Hours: poems (Cormorant, 2013)
The Temple (Baseline Press, 2018)
New Year Letter
(Baseline Press, 2020; second ed. 2021)
The Affirmations: poems (Biblioasis, 2022)
Membra Jesu nostri: a sung devotion
(with Daniel Cabena; Baseline Press, 2023)

AUTHOR PHOTO: KIRBY

LUKE HATHAWAY is an internationally-acclaimed poet, lyricist/librettist, and theatre-maker. Of his 2022 book *The Affirmations*, *Times* critic Graeme Richardson writes: "Mainstream poetry counts as non-conformist compared with popular culture, but it nevertheless develops its own conformities ... Luke Hathaway, a Canadian trans poet, offers ... a point of difference. Influenced by John Donne and George Herbert, and above all by T.S. Eliot's *Four Quartets*, Hathaway constructs small marvels of what one poem here calls 'loving jugglery': a feast of transformations." Hathaway is a co-creator of the immersive opera *Eurydice Fragments* (re:naissance opera, 2024), the song-cycle *The Sign of Jonas* (Milltown Records, 2024), and many other performance works. He teaches English and creative writing at Saint Mary's University.

MIX
Paper
FSC® C100212

Printed by Imprimerie Gauvin
Gatineau, Québec